Count

Jilly Hunt

www.raintreepublishers.co.uk
Visit our website to find out more information about Raintree books.

To order:

☎ Phone 0845 6044371
🖹 Fax +44 (0) 1865 312263
🖳 Email myorders@raintreepublishers.co.uk

Customers from outside the UK please telephone +44 1865 312262

Raintree is an imprint of Capstone Global Library Limited, a company incorporated in England and Wales having its registered office at 7 Pilgrim Street, London, EC4V 6LB – Registered company number: 6695582

Text © Capstone Global Library Limited 2012
First published in hardback in 2012
Paperback edition first published in 2013
The moral rights of the proprietor have been asserted.

Edited by Laura Knowles
Designed by Victoria Allen
Original illustrations © Capstone Global Library Ltd 2012
Illustrated by Oxford Designers and Illustrators
Picture research by Mica Brancic
Originated by Capstone Global Library Ltd 2012
Printed and bound in China by CTPS

ISBN 978 1 406 23579 1 (hardback)
15 14 13 12 11
10 9 8 7 6 5 4 3 2 1

ISBN 978 1 406 23586 9 (paperback)
16 15 14 13 12
10 9 8 7 6 5 4 3 2 1

British Library Cataloguing in Publication Data
Hunt, Jilly.
Russia. -- (Countries around the world)
947'.0863-dc22
A full catalogue record for this book is available from the British Library.

Acknowledgements
We would like to thank the following for permission to reproduce photographs: © Corbis p. 7; Corbis pp. 9 (© Hulton-Deutsch Collection), 10 (© Hulton-Deutsch Collection), 11 (© Hulton-Deutsch Collection), 12 (© Bettmann), 13 (Sygma/© Rick Maiman), 17 (© Gerd Ludwig), 28 (epa/© Sergei Chirikov), 30 (Lebrecht Music & Arts/© Lebrecht Authors), 31 (© Hulton-Deutsch Collection); Getty Images pp. 6 (Taxi/FPG), 26 (National Geographic/Gordon Wiltsie); iStockphoto p. 8 (© Nadezhda Bolotina), 33 (© Emiko Taki); Shutterstock pp. 5 (© ArtComma); Shutterstock pp. 15 (© Milevshi), 19 (© Pichugin Dmitry), 20 (© Belizar), 24 (© Sergiy Dontsov), 27 (© Petro Feketa), 29 (© S. Borisov), 34 (© Krechet), 35 (© Liseykina), 36 (© Mikhail Markovskiy), 46 (© Angilla S.).

Cover photograph of Tsarskoye selo, formerly Pushkin imperial estate, in St Petersburg, Russia reproduced with permission of Shutterstock/© Dainis Derics.

We would like to thank Daniel Block and Dr Mara Sukholutskaya for their invaluable help in the preparation of this book.

Every effort has been made to contact copyright holders of any material reproduced in this book. Any omissions will be rectified in subsequent printings if notice is given to the publisher.

Disclaimer
All the Internet addresses (URLs) given in this book were valid at the time of going to press. However, due to the dynamic nature of the Internet, some addresses may have changed, or sites may have changed or ceased to exist since publication. While the author and publisher regret any inconvenience this may cause readers, no responsibility for any such changes can be accepted by either the author or the publisher.

Contents

Some words are printed in bold, **like this**. You can find out what they mean by looking in the glossary.

Introducing Russia

What do you think of when you think of Russia? Russian dolls? Very cold winters? Siberia? The Cold War? **Communism**? Russia is a vast country with a fascinating history and a unique culture.

Russia is the largest country in the world. It has a great variety of landscapes and some impressive places. It has the deepest, oldest lake in the world; the biggest border of any country; and the longest river and the highest mountain in Europe.

Population

Over 140 million people live in Russia. Most of these are Russians. There are also more than 120 other **ethnic groups**, including Ukrainians, Bashkirs, Chuvashs, Uzbeks, Belarusians, Kazakhs, Azerbaijanis, and Tatars. Russia is a federation, which means that the country of Russia is made up of different regions and **republics** all under one government. Many of the ethnic groups are from these different regions or republics of Russia.

In the past, many people lived in **rural** areas, but now almost three quarters of the population live in **urban** areas. Russia's capital city is Moscow, and other main cities include St Petersburg, Novosibirsk, and Nizhny Novgorod.

A different alphabet

The Russian language uses the Cyrillic alphabet. This alphabet was developed by Greek **missionaries** who moved into Russia in the AD 980s. Russian is the official language of the country, but the different regions have their own languages, too.

How to say...

| hello | здра́вствуйте | (zdrah-stvuy-tyeh) |
| goodbye | досвидаія | (da svee-da-nyah) |

The Ural Mountains form the traditional divide between Europe and Asia.

History: tsars and revolutions

People have been living in Russia for a million years. Around 2,000 years ago, the **Slavic people** first settled in Russia. For centuries, Russia was ruled by a *tsar* or **emperor**, who has come from a family of rulers. The Russians view their first **dynasty** as having started in AD 862 with the leader Rurik.

The Romanov dynasty

In 1613, Mikail Romanov was elected as ruler. This was the beginning of the Romanov Dynasty, which was to rule until 1917 – just over 300 years! Russia became the largest **empire** in the world under the Romanov dynasty.

CATHERINE THE GREAT (1729-1796)

One of Russia's great rulers was Catherine the Great, who was only a Romanov by marriage. She was the wife of Peter III. People did not like Peter and his beliefs, and in July 1762 the army arrested him. Catherine became empress and took over the rule of the empire. She expanded Russia's territory even further.

Tsar Nicholas II was the last tsar to rule the Russian Empire. He is seen here with his family. The family was murdered by the **Bolsheviks** in July 1918. The location of their remains has been a mystery.

Russian Revolution

The last Romanov emperor was Nicholas II who **abdicated** in 1917. He was forced to abdicate because of a series of defeats. Russia's defeat in the Russo-Japanese War of 1904–1905 led to the Russian Revolution of 1905. Following this revolution, Nicholas agreed to have a government, but he eventually took most of their power away. During World War I, Russia lost more battles. These defeats led to rioting and to the **imperial** household being overthrown by another revolution in 1917.

This photo shows a parade of Bolshevik soldiers in the streets of Moscow in 1917. The Bolsheviks began ruling Russia following the 1917 revolution.

Formation of the USSR

Nicholas II lost control of Russia and the Bolshevik Party took over in 1917. This was a group of revolutionaries led by Vladimir Lenin. They established a communist government and withdrew Russia from World War I. They wanted to make society a fairer place. Under the *tsars*, the division of wealth was not equal. Some people were incredibly rich and other people were extremely poor. The communists believed that there should be a **communal** ownership of property.

In 1922 the communists formed a group of **republics**, called the **USSR** (Union of Soviet Socialist Republics). It became known as the Soviet Union. Russia was now called the Russian Federation, and was the largest of the republics. Other republics included Ukraine and Belorussia (now Belarus), and later Estonia, Latvia, Lithuania, and Uzbekistan.

Daily life

Life under the Bolsheviks remained tough. The three years of **civil war** that followed the end of the imperial family had exhausted Russia. Parts of the countryside had stopped sending food to the towns because **inflation** was so high that the money they got for it was not worth anything. In the cities, factories had to close because there were no **raw materials** to work with.

VLADIMIR ILYICH LENIN

(1870–1924)

Lenin was born as Vladimir Ilyich Ulyanov in Simbirsk, Russia on 22 April 1870. He decided to change his name to Lenin in 1901. Lenin took over the control of Russia in 1917. Although Lenin was fighting the cause for peasants and workers, he had little contact with them and could be merciless towards them. There was a great deal of suffering during his rule. The violent tactics he used were known as the "**Red Terror**". After two years of illness, Lenin died on 21 January 1924, aged 53.

The rise of Stalin

After Lenin died in 1924, there was a power struggle between Leon Trotsky and Joseph Stalin. Stalin won and forced Trotsky to leave the Soviet Union in 1929. Stalin ruled as a **dictator** and made many changes. He set about **industrializing** the USSR. For example, he forced peasants to work as employees on **collective farms**. The more wealthy farmers did not want collectivization to happen, so they resisted. The government seized their land and possessions. From 1932–1933, Stalin created a **famine** in Ukraine (part of the USSR) that killed between four and five million Ukrainian peasants.

JOSEPH STALIN

(1879–1953)

Stalin took control of the USSR in 1924 but he was worried that he would lose power. So he had a secret police force which he used to remove all his enemies. This period is known as the "Great Terror". Millions of people were killed. Estimates range from three million to more than ten million people.

Pact with Germany

Stalin was fearful of attack from **Nazi** Germany. Its leader, Adolf Hitler, wanted to destroy Soviet **communism**. However, in 1939, Stalin made a secret pact (promise) with Hitler that each country would not attack the other. This gave Stalin more time to build up his army. As a result of the pact, Hitler felt safe to invade Poland on 1 September 1939. This was the start of World War II.

After Hitler invaded Poland, Stalin invaded Finland and parts of eastern Europe. By 1941, Stalin and Hitler controlled most of Europe. In June 1941, Germany invaded the Soviet Union, breaking the secret pact between them. As a result, the Soviet Union joined the **allied forces**, led by the United States and Great Britain, to fight against Germany. The Soviet Union played a very important role in World War II, and Germany was finally defeated in 1945.

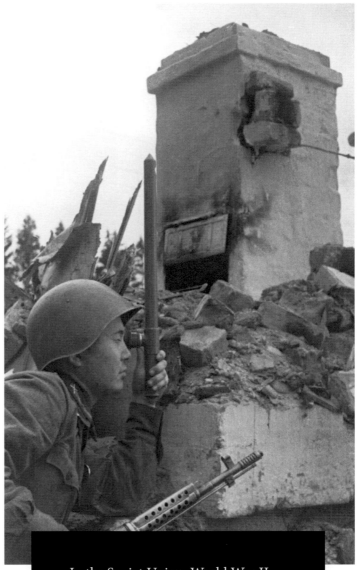

In the Soviet Union, World War II was known as the "Great Patriotic War". The Soviet Union suffered huge losses with more than 20 million soldiers and civilians killed.

The start of the Cold War

World War II changed Europe. Before the war, Germany was the greatest military power in Europe, but it was now defeated. The Soviet Union had suffered big losses but it still controlled almost all of eastern Europe. The Soviet Union set up communist governments in the countries it occupied. The United States and Great Britain had **democratic** governments and feared this rise in communism. This was the start of a long period of tension and competition between the United States and the Soviet Union known as the Cold War. They never fought each other directly but they would support opposing armies in struggles throughout the world.

Joseph Stalin died in 1953, after 29 years in power, and the worst era in Soviet history came to an end. There was more calm within the Soviet Union now.

End of the Cold War and the Soviet Union

Developments in the Soviet Union and changes in its leadership after Stalin's death led to the end of the Cold War. In 1985, Mikhail Gorbachev became head of the Communist Party. He introduced new policies which encouraged reforms but weakened the strength of the Communist Party. Power began to move to the individual republics that made up the Soviet Union. By the end of 1989, the eastern European countries had broken free of the Soviet Union. By the end of 1991, the Soviet Union had come to an end and Russia became an independent nation.

Daily life

The people of the Soviet Union were not able to speak freely against the government or help choose their leader. Gorbachev changed the rules of the Soviet government so that it allowed ordinary people to be involved in politics. He also allowed people to speak more freely and have access to more information.

Mikhail Gorbachev became General Secretary of the Communist Party in 1985, and President in 1988. He resigned as President in December, 1991, following the break up of the USSR.

Regions and resources: biggest, longest, coldest

Russia is the world's largest country, with an area of 17,098,200 square kilometres (6,601,700 square miles). Russia is almost twice as big as the United States or China. Russia lies partly on the continent of Europe and partly on the continent of Asia. The Ural Mountains which run north to south form the traditional boundary between Europe and Asia.

Russia covers most of eastern Europe and the whole of northern Asia. Russia has the longest border of any country in the world! This map shows the main physical features of the country.

Land height:

- Over 2000 metres
- Over 1000 metres
- Over 400 metres
- Over 200 metres
- Above sea level
- Below sea level
- Country borders

0 — 750 — 1500 kilometres
0 — 500 — 1000 miles

N

Arctic Ocean

SWEDEN
Baltic Sea
FINLAND
POLAND
ESTONIA
LATVIA
LITHUANIA
BELARUS
Lake Ladoga
Lake Onega
Ob
Arctic Circle
Lena
Kamchatka Peninsula
Kuril Islands
■ Moscow
UKRAINE
Ural Mountains
RUSSIA
SIBERIA
Volga
Black Sea
Caucasus Mts.
▲ Mount Elbrus
GEORGIA
ARMENIA
AZERBAIJAN
Caspian Sea
Irtysh
Yenisey
Amur
Lake Baikal
KAZAKHSTAN
Aral Sea
CHINA
JAPAN
NORTH KOREA
MONGOLIA
SOUTH KOREA
TURKMENISTAN
UZBEKISTAN
IRAN
Pacific Ocean

There are a number of active volcanoes on the Kamachatka Peninsula, in the far east of Russia.

REGIONS AND RESOURCES

Landscape

Around the Arctic Ocean, there are vast frozen plains known as tundra. The region of Siberia in northern Russia is mostly taiga, which are huge evergreen forests. West of the Ural Mountains it is mostly flat or **undulating** land. To the southeast, the land rises towards to the Caucasus Mountains. This is where Mount Elbrus is – Russia's highest point at 5,642 metres (18,510 feet). The Kamchatka Peninsula in the Russian Far East and the Kuril islands contain many active volcanoes.

Climate

The climate in Russia varies. In much of Russia it is continental. This means that summers can be hot and humid (damp) and winters are cold. However, the Arctic tundra and Siberia have extremely cold winters. Russia has the lowest temperature ever recorded outside Antactica of -71 °Celsius (-96 °Fahrenheit). This was recorded in the Siberian city of Oymyakon in 1926.

Agriculture

The climate in much of Russia is so harsh that only a relatively small area of land is farmed. Most of the farmland is used for growing crops, with the rest used for grazing animals. On the grasslands, crops such as wheat, barley, rye, and oats are grown. Beef cattle and pigs are raised. Millet and melons are grown along the lower Volga river.

YOUNG PEOPLE

The International Union of Young Farmers (IUYF) has been set up by the **United Nations (UN)**. The IUYF has an association in Russia. This group represents the interests of young farmers and young people living in **rural** areas. There are members of the IUYF from all over the world including Ireland, the United Kingdom, Germany, Austria, and Italy.

This map shows the population density of the various regions in Russia. Although only 25 per cent of the country lies west of the Ural Mountains, it is home to 80 per cent of the population.

People per square kilometre:
- 0.0–3.0
- 3.1–13
- 13.1–32
- 32.1–50
- 50.1–8,031.5
- Administrative borders
- Country borders

Resources

Russia has major deposits of oil, natural gas, and coal. Siberia is rich in coal, petroleum, natural gas, diamonds, iron ore, and gold. However, the harsh climate and huge distances make it very difficult to take advantage of these **natural resources**.

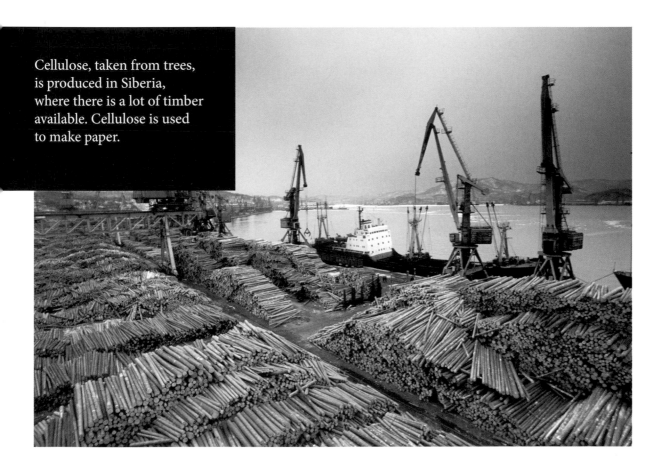

Cellulose, taken from trees, is produced in Siberia, where there is a lot of timber available. Cellulose is used to make paper.

Industry

There is a wide variety of industry in Russia, because of the natural resources available. For example, chemical industries have set up around the petroleum- and gas-producing areas in the Volga-Ural zone and the North Caucasus, and in areas served by **pipelines**. Electronic equipment, such as home appliances, is manufactured in areas where there are skilled workers, mainly in and around Moscow and St Petersburg.

Wildlife: protecting habitats

The plant and animal life in Russia varies depending on the landscape and climate. The tundra along northernmost Russia is frozen for most of the year. Only mosses, lichens, and grasses grow here. Animals such as reindeer, Arctic foxes, and musk oxen can also be found. In the taiga there are woodland animals such as squirrel, marten, fox, ermine, and sable. Elks, bears, muskrats, and wolves also make these forests their home. Marmots, skunks, foxes, and wolves live on the vast grasslands, called the steppes.

This herd of reindeer is looking for food under the snow near the Ural Mountains.

Russia's Lake Baikal has more than 1,700 **species** of plant and animal. About two thirds of these cannot be found anywhere else on Earth! A fish called golomyanka is unique to the lake. Unlike most fish, it gives birth to live young.

Climate change

Russia is the third biggest producer of **greenhouse gases**, after the United States and China. There are a lot of old industrial plants that pollute the environment. The process of extracting coal, oil, and petroleum causes further pollution. Greenhouse gases are the main cause of global warming and climate change. Russia is working to reduce the emission of greenhouse gases.

National parks and protected areas

Russia has a problem with environmental pollution, so many areas are protected under the country's nature reserve system. These protected areas are known as *zapovedniks* (zap-o-ved-niks). The first *zapovednik*, called Barguzinsky, was created in 1916 on the eastern shore of Lake Baikal. There are now 101 *zapovedniks* and 37 national parks. Altogether, more than 500,000 square kilometres (193,000 square miles) of land are protected.

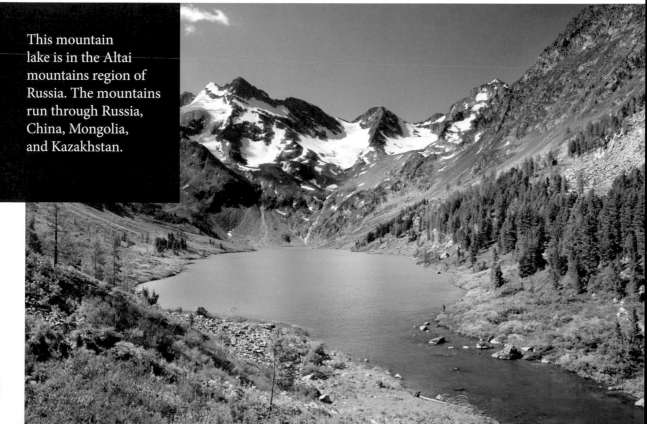

This mountain lake is in the Altai mountains region of Russia. The mountains run through Russia, China, Mongolia, and Kazakhstan.

Siberian tigers facing extinction

In the 1940s, the Siberian or Amur tiger was nearly **extinct**. There were no more than 40 Siberian tigers living in the wild. Most Siberian tigers are found in Russia, but there are also some in China. Russia has made a great effort to increase the numbers of tigers living in the wild by trying to stop **poaching**. In 2008, Russia created two new national parks to help protect the habitat of these rare tigers. The parks are in Primorsky Krai in the Russian Far East.

Now there are around 450 individual tigers living in the wild but they are still under threat because of continued poaching, increased **logging**, the building of new roads, and forest fires. The Cold War protected the Siberian tiger from hunting, as the areas where they lived were closed to most people. However, the collapse of the **USSR** led to a big increase in poaching as people tried to make money by supplying tiger parts for use in traditional Chinese medicine.

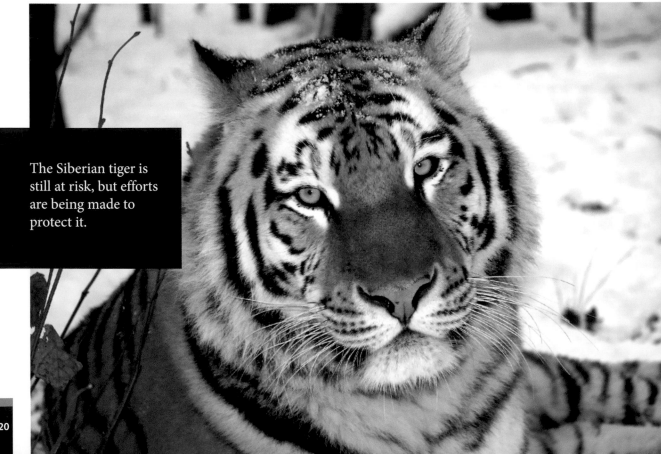

The Siberian tiger is still at risk, but efforts are being made to protect it.

In October 2010, the Siberian tigers' habitat was put under threat again. The forest administration of Primorsky Province in the Russian Far East announced that there would be an **auction** for logging rights in major tiger areas. The strong public outcry, both in Russia and the rest of the world, stopped the auction going ahead.

YOUNG PEOPLE

In November 2010, the **WWF** Tiger Youth Forum in Vladivostok had a video conference with the prime ministers of their countries who were attending the International Tiger Conservation Forum in St Petersburg. The young people asked them to try to double the wild tiger population by 2022. The Tiger Youth Forum is an international group working to protect tigers.

How to say...

bear	медведь	(myed-vyed)
fox	лиса	(leeh-sah)
reindeer	северный елень	(alen-sye-ver-nyyh ah-lehn)
squirrel	белка	(byel-kah)
wolf	волк	(volk)
mountain	ґора	(gah-rah)
forest	лес	(lyes)

Infrastructure: what makes Russia work?

A country's infrastructure is the set of systems and services that are needed for everyday life to run properly. The infrastructure includes transportation systems, schools, and hospitals. The Russian government runs the country.

Russia's full name is the Russian Federation. Being a federation means that the country is made up of regions that are partly self-governing, but also united by a central government. In the Russian Federation there are 83 administrative divisions, which include 21 republics. The republics have the right to have their own official language and have their own **constitution**.

This political map shows the different types of administrative division that make up the Russian Federation.

Type of administrative division:
- *Kray* (territory)
- *Oblast* (region)
- *Okrug* (autonomous district)
- Autonomous *oblast*
- Republic
- —— Administrative borders
- —— Country borders

| 0 | 750 | 1500 kilometres |
| 0 | 500 | 1000 miles |

N

Arctic Ocean

SWEDEN
Baltic Sea FINLAND
POLAND
ESTONIA
LATVIA • St. Petersburg
LITHUANIA
BELARUS

Arctic Circle

■ **Moscow**
• Nizhny Novgorod

UKRAINE

R U S S I A

• Rostov-na-Donu
Black Sea
• Pyatigorsk
• Yekaterinburg

• Khabarovsk

• Novosibirsk

GEORGIA
ARMENIA
AZERBAIJAN
Caspian Sea
TURKMENISTAN
UZBEKISTAN
IRAN

KAZAKHSTAN
Aral Sea

MONGOLIA

CHINA

JAPAN

NORTH KOREA

SOUTH KOREA

Pacific Ocean

Economic conditions

There have been major changes in the Russian **economy** since 1991. Before then, Russia was part of the USSR, and its economy was cut off from most of the world. Now the economy is part of the world economy. Russia exports a lot of goods to the rest of the world, so it can be affected if the price other countries will pay for these goods goes up or down. For example, when the price of oil dropped around the world in 2008–2009, the Russian economy was badly affected.

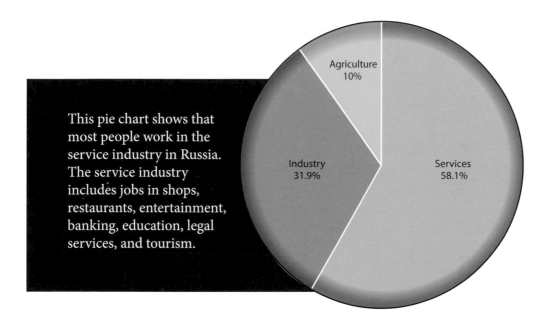

This pie chart shows that most people work in the service industry in Russia. The service industry includes jobs in shops, restaurants, entertainment, banking, education, legal services, and tourism.

Agriculture
10%

Industry
31.9%

Services
58.1%

Communications

Under the Soviet Union the government controlled all means of communication. The telephone system was used by the state to send military and government messages, rather than by ordinary people. Since 1991, there has been a great change in the telephone system in Russia. Now there is internet access and increased use of email.

Transportation

Russia relies on railways to cover its vast areas. Most of Russia's freight (goods) and about half of Russia's passengers travel by rail. There are more railway networks in some areas than others. The railways are controlled by the state.

Russia does have highways which link the major cities, but in general the road system is not very developed. The number of Russians owning a car is still small. In 2008, around 20 per cent of Russians owned a car. In the United States it is around 80 per cent.

Air transport is becoming more important in Russia. Not much freight is carried by plane, except for expensive items that need to go to and from remote parts of Siberia. Sometimes planes are the only means of transport here.

The railway is an important way for people to travel around Russia.

Housing

During the time of the Soviet Union, nearly all houses were owned by the state. Private property was banned in **urban** areas and the size of private homes was controlled in **rural** areas. In urban areas, most people lived in high-rise apartment buildings. Rents were kept very low and in most cases did not cover maintenance costs. Many apartment buildings are now in a bad state of repair. The government is supporting new home-building schemes and old buildings are being pulled down.

Daily life

In the Soviet era many people in Moscow lived in **communal** apartments called *communalki*. These apartments had kitchens and bathrooms that had to be shared between a number of families. Now many people in Moscow want to live in new homes, where they do not have to share facilties.

Healthcare

Basic healthcare is free to most of the population. However, public healthcare has deteriorated since the Soviet era. This is partly due to lack of funding, medicine shortages, and lack of properly trained medical staff. The government has made it a priority to improve healthcare. Some of the measures they want to take include the training or retraining of doctors, increasing wages, purchasing more equipment, and increasing **immunizations**. Russia is facing one of the fastest growing epidemics of HIV/AIDS in the world. The number of cases of people dying from tuberculosis is also high, and could be improved with an immunization programme.

Education

Many children in Russia go to nursery or pre-school, but it is not **compulsory**. Free, compulsory education starts when a child is seven years old. Children must go to school for at least eight years to gain a basic general education certificate. To get the secondary-level certificate, children must spend an additional two or three years at school. Many children go on to higher education. There are more than 8.5 million students in higher education.

School starts at about 8.00 a.m and finishes at 1.00 or 2.00 p.m. Children can take part in after-school activities such as dancing, sports, singing, or painting. School runs from Monday to Friday and children either walk to school or take public transport. Most children buy hot school lunches, rather than bringing their own from home. At school, children learn subjects such as Russian, mathematics, social sciences, humanities, and the arts.

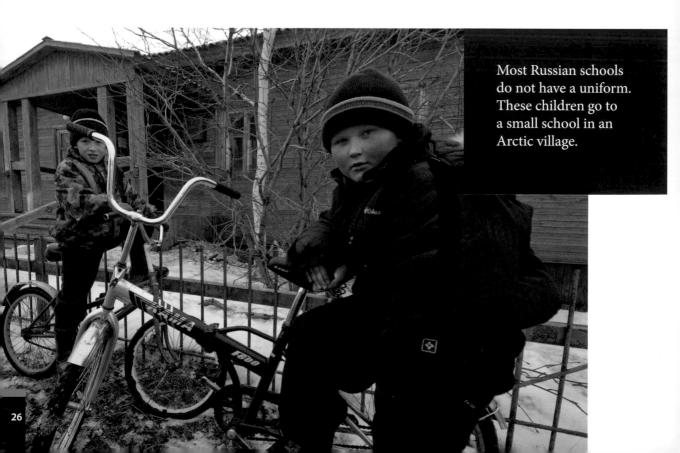

Most Russian schools do not have a uniform. These children go to a small school in an Arctic village.

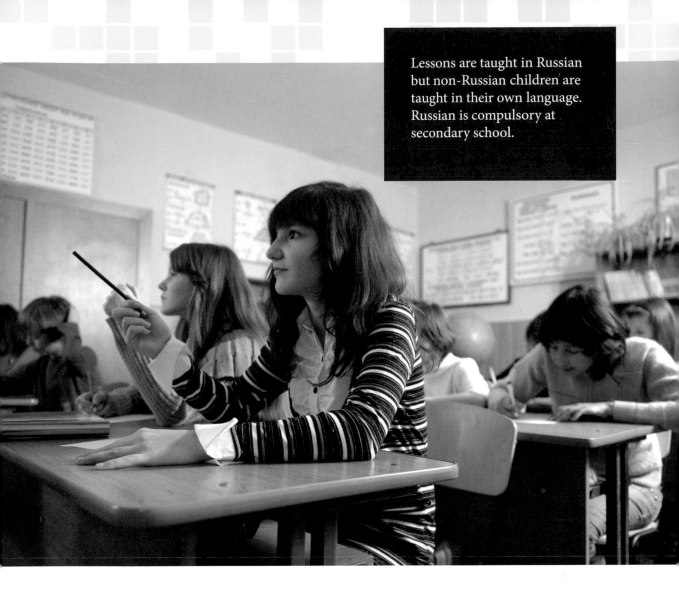

Lessons are taught in Russian but non-Russian children are taught in their own language. Russian is compulsory at secondary school.

How to say...

book	книга	(knee-gah)
class	класс	(klahss)
school	школа	(shkoh-lah)
language	язык	(yah-zyk)
lunch	обед	(ah-byed)
teacher	учитель	(ooh-chee-tel)

Culture: myths, tradition, and revival

Russia has no official religion. Before **communism**, the Russian Orthodox Church played a major part in Russian culture and there has been a return to it now. Islam is the second largest religion in Russia. This dates back to when Russia was controlled by the Muslim Tatars in the 1200s.

Festivals and holidays

New Year is a big celebration in Russia because under the communists people were not allowed to celebrate religious festivals. New Year became the new way of celebrating Christmas. Now, since the majority of people in Russia are Christian, Christmas and Easter are also important occasions.

Daily life

One special occasion is *Maslenitsa*, or Pancake Week. This is a week of feasting before Lent to mark the end of winter. There are celebrations held all over Russia and of course pancakes are eaten!

These Russian girls are performing a dance during the celebrations of *Maslenitsa*. They are wearing traditional Russian costumes.

Art

A famous Russian artist is the goldsmith and jeweller Karl Fabergé. He is well known for his highly decorative enamel Easter eggs made for the Russian royal family. Vasily Kandinsky is another very famous Russian artist. He was one of the leading figures in **abstract art** and his work can be seen around the world.

Some of the world's most famous museums are found in Moscow and St Petersburg. For example, the Pushkin Fine Arts Museum and the Hermitage in St Petersburg.

The Kremlin in Moscow used to be the home of the Russian president and the centre of communist power. Now it contains some important museums. The Kremlin building is a work of art in its own right.

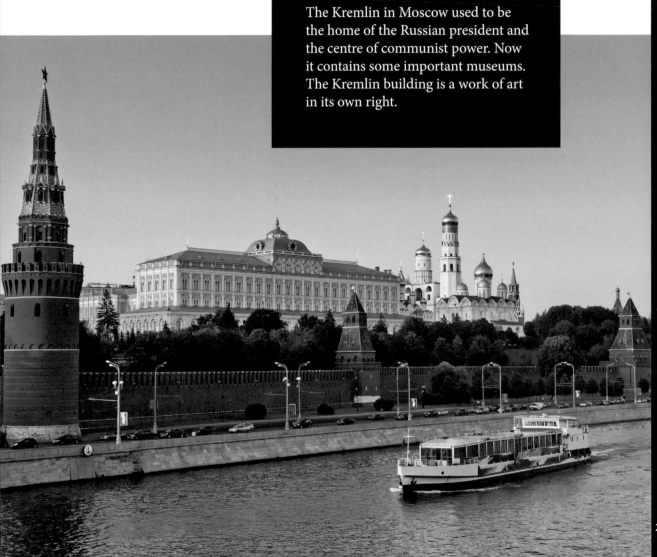

Literature

There are many famous Russian poets and novelists throughout history. Two well-respected authors are Fyodor Dostoevsky and Leo Tolstoy. Dostoevsky wrote *Crime and Punishment* in 1866. Tolstoy is best known for his novels *War and Peace* (1865–69) and *Anna Karenina* (1875–77). Anton Chekhov is a famous Russian playwright. He wrote plays such as *The Seagull* (1896) and *The Cherry Orchard* (1904). Aleksandr Pushkin is thought by many to be one of Russia's greatest poets, novelists and playwrights. His famous works include *Eugene Onegin* (1833) and *Boris Godunov* (1831).

Leo Tolstoy is often thought of as one of the world's greatest novelists. He was born in 1828 and died in 1910.

Music

Piotr Illyich Tchaikovsky (1840–1893) is Russia's most famous composer. He is probably best known for his 1812 overture, as well as for composing music for ballets. Another famous Russian compser was Nikolay Rimsky-Korsakov (1844–1908), who wrote "The Flight of the Bumblebee".

Russian ballet

Russia is well known for its ballet. The first ballet school was opened in 1734. In 1847 a French dancer and **choreographer** called Marius Petipa established St Petersburg as a centre for the best ballet dancers and choreographers. Petipa worked with the Russian Imperial Ballet for nearly 60 years on many famous ballets including *Swan Lake*, *Sleeping Beauty,* and *The Nutcracker*. The music for these three ballets was written by Tchaikovsky.

In 1909, a new, inventive touring ballet company called Ballet Russe was founded by Sergey Diaghilev. The Ballet Russe toured Europe, and North and South America.

ANNA PAVLOVA
(1881–1931)

Anna Pavlova was the most celebrated dancer of her time. She was born into Tsarist Russia, which had excellent schools for the performing arts. Anna was accepted into the Imperial School of Ballet in St Petersburg in 1891. Her talent shone through and she went on to tour the world.

Sport

Sport plays an important part in Russian life. Many Russian sports stars have become famous all over the world, for example, tennis players Anna Kournikova and Maria Sharapova. Anna has reached number eight in the World Tennis Association rankings. Maria became the third youngest female to win at Wimbledon in 2004, when she beat defending champion Serena Williams.

Russia has also enjoyed success in gymnastics, figure skating, and ice hockey. Russian players have been particularly strong in ice hockey. As in many countries around the world, football is very popular. One of the most famous players is the goalkeeper Lev Yashin. He helped Russia win the gold medal in the 1956 Olympics. Yashin died in 1990, and in his honour **FIFA** established the Yashin Award for the Best Goalkeeper in 1994. Recently, Russian football has been helped by an investment of millions of pounds by Roman Abramovich, a Russian businessman who owns Chelsea Football Club in the United Kingdom.

Russia is also well known for its successful chess players. Famous Russian chess players include Alexander Alekhine, Garry Kasparov and Vladimir Kramnik.

Daily life

There is a lack of sporting facilities and equipment in much of Russia, so many people take part in jogging, football and fishing, because these sports do not need much equipment.

Food

Western-style food is popular in Russia but the Russian traditions are still strong. One of the traditional favourites is *blini* which are like pancakes. *Blini* can be eaten at breakfast or as part of an appetizer (*zakuski*) with **caviar** (*ikra*), sour cream or salmon. Russians usually have their main meal at lunchtime.

Blini

Ingredients

- 2 eggs
- 1 tablespoon white sugar
- 1/3 teaspoon salt
- 50 grams plain flour
- 500 millilitres milk
- 1 tablespoon vegetable oil
- 1 tablespoon butter

What to do

1. Whisk the eggs, sugar, and salt in a medium-sized bowl.
2. Sift the flour into the bowl, and stir in the egg mixture along with the milk.
3. Mix until smooth. The batter should be thin.

Cooking the *blini*

4. Heat a frying pan over a medium heat. You should ask an adult to help you.
5. Lightly oil the pan.
6. When the oil is hot, pour about 2 tablespoons of the batter into the pan.
7. Spread the batter out evenly by tilting the pan.
8. Cook until the edges look crisp and the centre appears dry.
9. Slide a spatula under the blini and flip it over.
10. Cook for about 1 minute, or until lightly brown.
12. Remove the *blini* from the pan and onto a plate.
13. Put a little butter on top and continue to stack the *blini* until all the batter has been used.

Russia today

Russia's **economy** went through a difficult time during the global economic crisis of 2008–2009 but the economy is recovering. Russia still faces many challenges. A lot of money is needed to improve schools, hospitals, and roads. There is still a large difference between the wealth of people living in cities and people living in **rural** areas.

In 2010, Russia and the **European Union (EU)** agreed that Russia should enter the **World Trade Organization**. This means that Russia will be able to trade more freely with other countries across the world. International companies will come to Russia to produce goods, which will create jobs for Russian people. Russian companies will have to become more competitive if they are going to succeed against international companies but if they can, they have the chance to sell their goods all over the world.

Although they are surrounded by beautiful landscape, the people in Russian villages are often poorer than those in the cities.

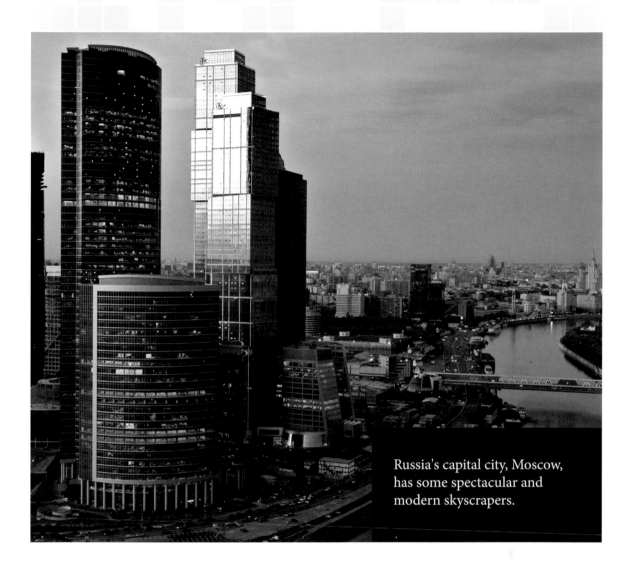

Russia's capital city, Moscow, has some spectacular and modern skyscrapers.

In December 2010, **FIFA** announced that Russia would be the host country for the 2018 Football World Cup. This is the first time an eastern European country will host the event. The announcement is exciting for Russia because it means that there will be a lot of investment in the country. In order to host the tournament Russia will have to build 16 stadiums, lots of hotels and airports, and hundreds of kilometres of roads. This will be an expensive job. It is expected that nearly £7 billion will need to be invested in the tourist industry alone. The tournament in 2018 will leave behind it some great new facilities for the Russian people.

Fact file

Official long name: Russian Federation

Official short name: Russia

Official language: Russian

Population: 138,739,900 (2011 estimate)

Currency: ruble

Capital city: Moscow

Area: 17,098,200 square kilometres (6,601,700 square miles)

Bordering countries: Azerbaijan, Belarus, China, Estonia, Finland, Georgia, Kazakhstan, North Korea, Latvia, Lithuania, Mongolia, Norway, Poland, Ukraine

Rivers: Russia's longest rivers are the Ob-Irtysh, Amur, Lena and Yenisey rivers. These rivers run through Siberia.

There are more than 100,000 rivers in Russia. The Volga is the most important river in European Russia. It is the longest river in Europe, at 3,530 kilometres (2,193 miles), and is a major trade route.

Largest lake: : Lake Ladoga – 17,350 square kilometres (6,700 square miles)

Deepest lake: Lake Baikal. Maximum depth of 1620 metres (5315 feet). It is the deepest and oldest existing freshwater lake on Earth and is thought to be 20 to 25 million years old.

Highest point: Mount Elbrus at 5,642 metres (18,510 feet). This is also Europe's highest peak.

Lowest point: Caspian Sea at -28 metres (-92 feet)

Temperatures:	Russia has the world's lowest temperature recorded outside of Antarctica -71 °Celsius (-96 °Fahrenheit)
Poverty rate:	13.1 per cent of Russia's population live below the poverty line
Main exports:	petroleum and petroleum products, natural gas, grain, wood and wood products, metals, and chemicals
Main imports:	vehicles, machinery and equipment, plastics, medicines, iron and steel, consumer goods, meat, fruit, and nuts, and semi-finished metal products
Main trading partners:	Netherlands, Italy, Germany, China, Turkey, Ukraine, and the United States

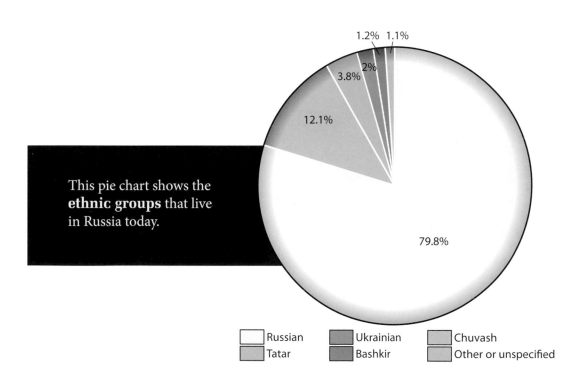

This pie chart shows the **ethnic groups** that live in Russia today.

1.2% 1.1%
2%
3.8%
12.1%
79.8%

☐ Russian   ▨ Ukrainian   ▨ Chuvash
▨ Tatar   ▨ Bashkir   ☐ Other or unspecified

Official state holidays:

New Year's Day – 1 January
Christmas Day – 7 January
Defender of the Motherland Day –
    23 February
International Women's Day – 8 March
Labour Day – 1 May
Victory Day – 9 May
Russia Day – 12 June
National Unity Day – 4 November

Christmas Day is not on the 25 December. This is because the Russian Orthodox Church uses a different calendar, which is 12 days behind the one used in western countries.

Famous Russians :

Tsar Peter I, called Peter the Great (1672–1725). Peter ruled from 1682 to 1725 and made Russia stronger. He made changes to the government and built a new capital city, which he called St Petersburg.

Modest Mussorgsky (1839–1881) – composer

Konstantin Sergeyevick Stanislavsky (1863–1938) – actor, director and producer

Sergey Prokofiev (1891–1953) – composer

Dmitry Shostakovich (1906–1975) – composer

Yury Gagarin (1934–1968) – astronaut

Rudolf Nureyev (1938–93) – ballet dancer

Valentina Matvienko (born 1949) – governor of St Petersburg

Vladimir Putin (born 1952) – Russia's second president from 1999–2008, prime minister from 2008

Tatyana Golikova (born 1966) – Health and Social Development Minister in the Russian government

Andrey Arshavin (born 1981) – footballer

Alexander Ovechkin (born 1985) – ice hockey player who played in the 2010 Winter Olympics

National anthem:

Russia's national anthem was adapted from the music of the Soviet Union's anthem, with words by Sergey Mikhalkov. Below is an English translation.

Russia – our holy nation,
Russia – our beloved country.
A mighty will, great glory –
These are yours for all time!

Chorus:
Be glorious, our free Motherland,
Age-old union of fraternal peoples,
Popular wisdom given by our forebears!
Be glorious, our country! We are proud of you!

From the southern seas to the polar lands
Spread our forests and fields.
You are unique in the world, one of a kind –
Native land protected by God!

Chorus

Wide spaces for dreams and for living
Are opened for us by the coming years
Our loyalty to our Motherland gives us strength.
Thus it was, thus it is and always will be!

Chorus

Timeline

BC is short for "before Christ". BC is added after a date and means that the date occurred before the birth of Jesus Christ, for example, 450 BC.

AD is short for *Anno Domini*, which is Latin for "in the year of our Lord". AD is added before a date and means that the date occurred after the birth of Jesus Christ, for example, AD 720.

AD 862	Rurik becomes leader of Russia and starts the first Russian **dynasty**
1613	Mikail Romanov is elected to rule and is the first ruler of the Romanov Dynasty
1734	The first ballet school opens in Russia
1762	The Russian army arrests Tsar Peter III
	Tsar Peter III's wife, Catherine, becomes ruler of Russia. She will later become known as Catherine the Great.
1796	Catherine the Great dies
1865–1869	Leo Tolstoy writes *War and Peace*
1866	Fyodor Dostoevsky writes *Crime and Punishment*
1875–1877	Tolstoy writes *Anna Karenina*
1896	Anton Chekov writes *The Seagull*
1905	The Russian Revolution takes place
1909	The Ballet Russe is founded
1916	The first *zapovednik* (nature reserve) is created on the eastern shore of Lake Baikal

1917	The last Russian tsar, Tsar Nicholas II, **abdicates**
	The second Russian Revolution leads to the Bolshevik Party seizing control of Russia. Lenin takes control.
1918	Bolsheviks murder tsar Nicholas II and his family
1922	The **USSR** (Union of Soviet Socialist **Republics**) is founded
1924	Lenin dies of a stroke
	Joseph Stalin seizes power of the Communist Party and the USSR. His time in power becomes known as the "Great Terror"
1932–1933	**Famine** in Ukraine kills four to five million peasants
1939	Stalin and Hitler make a secret pact not to attack each other
	Hitler invades Poland and World War II begins
1941	Germany invades the USSR, breaking Hitler's pact with Stalin
1945	Germany is defeated and World War II ends
1953	Stalin dies
1985	Mikhail Gorbachev becomes head of the Communist Party and changes the law, allowing ordinary people to speak more freely and be involved in politics
1988	Gorbachev becomes president of the USSR
1989	Eastern European countries leave the USSR
1991	The Soviet Union ends and Russia becomes an independent nation. Gorbachev resigns.
2010	**FIFA** announces that Russia will host the 2018 Football World Cup.

Glossary

abdicate give up right to the throne

abstract art art that tries to show ideas rather than the way things look

allied forces military forces of a group of countries, including Russia, the UK, and the USA, who fought against Germany in World War II

auction sale in which goods or property is sold to the person who bids (offers) the highest amount of money

Bolsheviks division of Social Democrats led by Lenin

caviar eggs of a large fish, eaten as a delicacy

choreographer person who plans out the steps a dance

civil war war between people of the same country

collective farm farm in which land and tools are owned by the state rather than by an individual

communal shared or done by all members of a group

communism political theory which believes in state ownership of goods for the benefit of all. A supporter of communism is called a communist.

compulsory required or demanded

democratic system of government

dictator leader who has complete power in a country and has not been elected by the people

dynasty family of rulers

economy relating to the money, industry, and jobs in a country

emperor ruler of an empire

empire group of states or countries under one ruler

ethnic group group of people sharing the same national or cultural traditions

European Union (EU) international organization of European countries with shared political and economic aims. The EU formed from the EEC (European Economic Community) in 1993.

extinct die out completely

famine large-scale lack of food over a wide area, leading to starvation

FIFA International Federation of Association Football. The governing body of football.

greenhouse gases gases, such as carbon dioxide, that trap the Sun's energy and makes Earth warm up

immunization vaccination

imperial royal

industrializing make more industrial

inflation rise in prices

logging cutting and preparing forest timber

missionaries people who travel to a foreign country to do religious or charitable work

natural resource thing that exists naturally and is used by people, such as coal, oil, or forests

Nazi member of the National Socialist Party in Germany during Hitler's time

pipelines pipes that take gas or oil to where it is needed

poaching hunting and catching animals illegally

raw material natural substance that other things are made from

Red Terror mass excecutions of political opponents of Lenin

republic country with an elected government and a president instead of a king or queen

rural to do with the countryside

Slavic people people from central and eastern Europe who speak a Slavonic language, such as Russian

species category in the classification system; group of a particular type

undulating having a wavy surface or shape

United Nations (UN) international organization set up in 1945 to promote international peace

urban to do with a town or city

USSR stands for Union of Soviet Socialist Republics, also called the Soviet Union. The USSR was an empire in which communist Russia controlled neighbouring countries from 1917 to 1991

World Trade Organization international body whose aim is to get countries to trade more freely with each other by getting rid of duties and barriers

WWF charity that used to be known as the World Wildlife Fund for Nature. The WWF helps to protect endangered animals and habitats.

Find out more

Books

R is for Russia (World Alphabet), Vladimir Kabakov (Frances Lincoln, 2011)
Russia (Changing World), Simon Adams (Franklin Watts, 2010)
Russia in Pictures (Visual Geography Series), Heron Marquez
    (Lerner Books, 2009)
Russia (Looking at Countries), Jillian Powell (Franklin Watts, 2006)
The Russian Revolution (20th Century Perspectives), Tony Allan
    (Heinemann Library, 2002)

DVDs

Nicholas and Alexandra (Sony Pictures Home Entertainment, 2002)
This film tells the story of Nicholas II, the last tsar of Russia.

October 1917 – Ten Days that Shook the World (Eureka Entertainment, 2000)
The director of this film had been commissioned by Lenin to make a film commemorating the 10th anniversary of the government being overthrown by the Bolsheviks.

The Russian Revolution in Colour (Demand Media Limited, 2008)
Details the events leading up to the Russian Revolution of 1917.

Websites

www.wild-russia.org/default.htm
Find out more about Russian nature conservation.

kids.nationalgeographic.com/kids/places/find/russia
This website contains facts about Russia and plenty of photos. It also includes a short video about Russia's volcanoes.

Places to visit

If you ever get the chance to go to Russia, here are some interesting places to visit:

Red Square, Moscow

Here, you can see St Basil's Cathedral, The Kremlin, and Lenin's Mausoleum.

Pushkin Museum of Fine Arts, Moscow

This museum contains a famous collection of Impressionist and Post-Impressionist paintings. It also has an exhibition of controversial paintings stolen from European Jews by the Nazis, that were rescued by Soviet troops.

The Hermitage, St Petersburg

This art collection is housed in the palace from which the tsars ruled the Russian Empire.

Church of Our Saviour on Spilled Blood (Spas na Kravi), St Petersburg

This beautiful, old style Russian church has spectacular blue and gold onion-shaped domes. and is filled with spectacular mosaics.

Topic tools

You can use these topic tools for your school projects. Trace the map on to a sheet of paper, using the black outline to guide you.

Russia's flag has three equal horizontal bands of white, blue, and red. There is no official meaning behind these colours. Copy the flag design and then colour in your picture. Make sure you use the right colours!

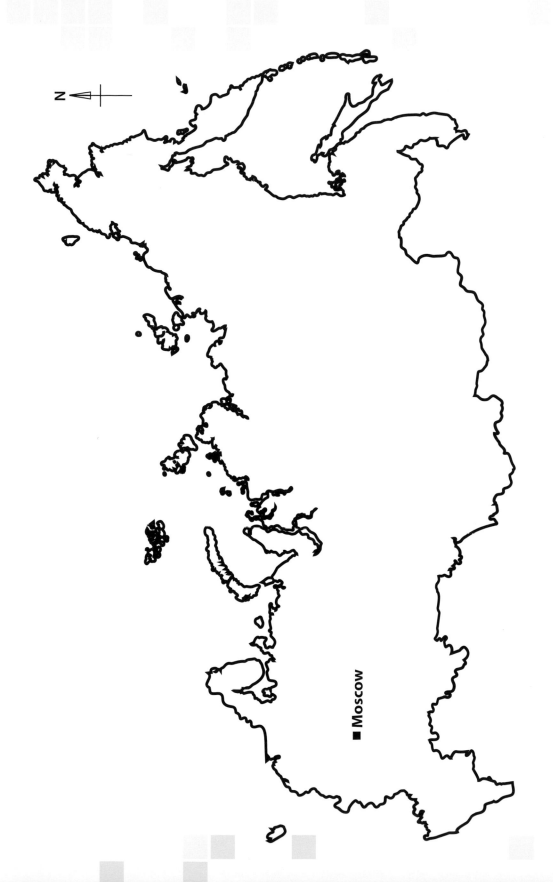

■ Moscow

Index